OFF ON A
TANGENT

Bob Stutman

Rom. 8:28

OFF ON A TANGENT

A SURVEY OF SOUND DOCTRINE GONE WILD

". . . 'If you abide in My word, you are My disciples indeed. And you shall know the truth, and the truth shall make you free.'"

John 8:31b & 32

BOB SCHWANDT

Charleston, SC
www.PalmettoPublishing.com

OFF ON A TANGENT

First Edition

Hardcover ISBN: 978-1-64990-773-8
Paperback ISBN: 978-1-64990-774-5
eBook ISBN: 978-1-64990-775-2

I dedicate this book to the memory of my late wife of 53 years, Phyllis.

LET ME HEAR YOUR VOICE

BOB SCHWANDT

*Many voices clamor for attention
It's so hard to know which path to take;
Wisdom of this world does not seem to fill the void;
Then I look to you, Lord, for the only path to take;*

*Let me hear your voice; Lord I need to hear from you;
Whisper to my heart the things you need from me;
Speak in words so clear, that I know it's you, dear Lord;
I will honor what I hear you speak to me.*

*In this day and age, we are now living,
Man has drifted far from God's great plan;
Bible truth is lost; they say foolish is the cross.
Many don't believe that God's still reaching out to man.*

*Let me hear your voice; Lord I need to hear from you;
Whisper to my heart the things you need from me;
Speak in words so clear, that I know it's you, dear Lord;
I will honor what I hear you speak to me.*

INTRODUCTION

I have been a minister of the Gospel (now retired) for many years, and at one point in my ministry, I sensed that God wanted me to write the book that I am presenting to you.

Christian beliefs based on contextual Scripture is the basis for healthy growth of a believer and of the church. I hasten to add that I see a great difference between two terms as used in Scripture: *The Assembly*, which denotes the local congregation or an association of local congregations as opposed to *the church*, which is the universal body of believers. Unfortunately, the two terms are used interchangeably, causing much confusion. If a person is a member of a local congregation, such as Baptist, Lutheran, Catholic, Assemblies of God, etc., they are assumed to be a part of *the church*, the universal Body of Christ, but there is no scriptural basis for such a belief. In fact, it leads to much confusion. Does this mean that I am opposed to organized religion or denominations? No, of course not.

When asked if a person is a Christian, the answer is often, "Yes, of course. I am a member in good standing in a local assembly". Often, this signifies that a person's security may be in an organization, and not in Christ. The Christian's faith *must* be in Christ rather than in a religious organization or system! Many nominal church members believe that they are ready for the taking away of the church (rapture), and they may be shocked when millions are suddenly missing and they are left behind. I hope in some small way that this book will help to awaken many to the fact that a relationship with Christ, not just active involvement in a local congregation, is needed to be caught away in the rapture of the church.

Accordingly, it is then possible that many Sunday School Teachers, deacons, choir members, worship leaders, preachers, and many more may be serving a local assembly and may not really be involved in a personal relationship with Jesus Christ. In Matthew's Gospel, we read, "Not everyone who says to Me, 'Lord, Lord,' will enter the kingdom of heaven but he who does the will of my Father who is in heaven. Many will say to Me on that day, 'Lord, Lord, did we not prophesy in your name, and in your name cast out demons, and your name perform many miracles?' And then I will declare to them, 'I never knew you; depart from Me, you who practice lawlessness!" (Matthew 7:21–23) A person can be actively involved in a local assembly, and yet not know Jesus Christ.

Some of you may feel that I am being judgmental with my remarks, but I don't think so. I believe that I am acting as a watchman. God is the judge, not me, nor any other Christian. It is important that a person becomes aware of what Scripture says, and that they are warned of deviations from the truth as presented in the Bible. I leave you to evaluate and decide for yourself what is true and what is false. In this presentation, I will deal with what I call "tangent teachings" (a solid biblical doctrine that is taken to the extreme) that are causing many to be misled and to fail to live successful Christian lives. As I list some of these, many flags may go up based on traditional teachings and beliefs, but let me quickly say that every *tangent* that I present in this book is based on solid, Scripture-based doctrine. They are rooted in the Word of God, but when taken to an extreme, they take the believer from the complete central truth of the Word, leaving the believer dangling *off on a tangent*. If you see me dealing with a pet doctrine of your belief system, please don't stop reading. I encourage you to see what I am saying *in the context of Scripture.*

I will be dealing with various themes that have become excessive and have drifted away from the central theme of Scripture, which is God's love and His only begotten Son who was given as a ransom for sin. This is the main theme of the Bible from Genesis through Revelation. We find types of Christ in the old testament and fulfillment, or antitypes, in the new testament. I propose to show that the doctrinal excesses, though true in their contextual focus, have distracted from the main theme of the Bible, which is God's redemption of man. Various themes such as the gifts of the Spirit, praise and worship, music, evangelism, and many, many other things are indeed scriptural and correct for the church today, but often are emphasized so much, by themselves, that they can lead us away from the central truth of God's Word, which, again, is Jesus, the Love of God, etc. The tangents become the main theses or emphasis, and the central truths are somewhere in the shadows. I will explain this in more detail when dealing with the various tangents. In no way is this intended to be an exhaustive study on the subject, but rather a primer of sorts. If after considering what I will be presenting you want to toss out the entire book, please feel free to do so. I will have accomplished my part in what I believe that God has been leading me to do for many years. I would hope, rather, that your appetite for truth will be challenged to the point that you further research this topic on your own. May God richly bless and inspire you with this presentation.

Prayerfully,
Bob Schwandt

Please note: Unless otherwise stated, all Scripture quotes are from the New American Standard Version

(NASB) of the Bible.

1

WHAT IS A TANGENT?

I am dealing with the word "tangent" in this book, but first, let's discuss what I mean by that term. According to Merriam-Webster, one definition of tangent is: "meeting a curve or a surface in a single point of a sufficiently small interval is considered"

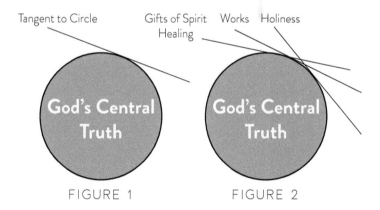

Tangent to Circle   Gifts of Spirit   Works Holiness
Healing

God's Central Truth   **God's Central Truth**

FIGURE 1   FIGURE 2

You see in the illustration two circles: The first simply illustrates what a single tangent is. The second shows how several Bible truths are illustrated as many tangents to

God's Central Truth. (I have indicated three tangents; however, there are many more.) Where the tangent touches the circle, it relates to God's Central Truth. When we move away on the tangent or "go off on a tangent," it is removed from God's Central Truth and is creating a theme not fully related to the whole counsel of God's Word.

This will all be explained in greater detail as we get into the various tangents of doctrines. Suffice to say, no matter which truth we emphasize, *we must never remove that belief from the Central Truth of God's Word, which reflects God's love for His creation and God's precious gift to a lost world, His only begotten Son, Jesus.* In the following chapters, we will present some of the more obvious excesses that are causing harm to the Body of Christ, and we will try to correctly place their priority where it should be for the church to be healthy and strong.

2

DIVINE HEALING

When God made the first human beings, He placed them in the Garden of Eden, according to the Book of Genesis. He loved Adam and Eve and provided His best for them. The Bible gives us a picture of a beautiful Paradise, unmarred in any way. It was perfect. He gave them some very basic instructions. The whole area was theirs to enjoy. Everything was theirs. They could eat of any tree in that beautiful place of perfection, with one important exception: The one thing that they could not touch was the fruit of the tree of the knowledge of good and evil. God told them that if they did partake of the fruit of that tree, they would surely die.

Well, Genesis tells us that they disobeyed God. The serpent (Satan) enticed Eve to eat of that tree, and when she realized that it was pleasant to eat, Eve shared the fruit with Adam. Satan had lied by telling them that they would not die, as God had said, but they would become as gods themselves, knowing the difference between good and evil. Satan always presents *half-truths* in an attempt to legitimize what he tells us.

It was God's practice to enjoy daily fellowship with man, so later that day, God came to the garden, but they were hiding from Him because they knew that they were naked, and were ashamed. They had been disobedient to God's instruction, and as a result, God placed a curse on the serpent (Satan), who tempted Eve, and also on the earth and on mankind. Until that point, they had known only perfection and beauty, but that all changed. They were no longer allowed to remain in the garden and were banned from ever returning to it. Instead, they would find that life would take on a whole new perspective. They would no longer live a life of ease but would have to toil and labor for all they would need. Sin and death had entered the world through their disobedience, and they would be subject to sin's fruit: pain, suffering, disappointment, disease, illness, and death.

God, however, had a plan to redeem man from the sin that their disobedience had brought to the world. As we look at the history of God's chosen people, the Jews, we see a picture of God's final act that would remove the result of sin from His creation: The blood sacrifice of the lamb (Exodus 12) and later the annual sacrifice with the blood being sprinkled on the mercy seat, the golden cover of the ark of the covenant in the Holy of Holies of the tabernacle, which would cover, but not forgive, the sins of Israel (Leviticus 16:30, Hebrews 9:22). God's forgiveness of sin was to be completed later in the intimate, one time, sacrifice of the perfect Lamb of God, Jesus, on the cross. John the Baptist, referring to Jesus said, "Behold the Lamb of God who takes away the sin of the world"(John 1:29)

We read in Psalm 103:2–3, "Bless the Lord, O my soul, And forget none of His benefits; Who pardons all your iniquities, Who heals all your diseases;" and we see in James 5:14–15, "Is anyone among you sick? Let him call for the elders of the church and let them pray over him, anointing him with oil in the name of the Lord; and the prayer offered in faith will restore the one who is sick, and the Lord will raise him up, and if he has committed sins, they will be forgiven him", and there are many other Scriptures in both the old and new testament that clearly state that we can believe God for physical healing. Of course, the final healing will take place when the church victoriously will rise to meet the Lord at the rapture. Until that blessed day, if we are true to the Word of God, we can trust God for physical healing as well as spiritual healing. So be aware that the final release from the curse of sin in this world will totally come at the end of the age when the church will rise to meet Jesus and be with Him for eternity. Death and sin, and the effects of sin, will be totally destroyed. Until then, we have the provision to believe God for healing of sin and sickness because of Christ's sacrifice.

So, what do we do to receive physical healing? First of all, I firmly believe that God has blessed us with medical science to affect healing for us. In the New Testament, Paul, the Apostle refers to Luke as the beloved physician (Col 4:14), so there is obviously no negative connotation there regarding medical science. He was a doctor of physical healing. The important thing to realize is that God can, and will, heal in our day and age through natural means (which He inspired) and also through supernatural means. But before we go further, let's deal with the extreme *tangent* of healing—the fact that we do not always receive healing when we pray for it. Read on.

In the first half of the twentieth century, we witnessed a great interest in the ministry of physical healing. As a young boy, I went with my parents to meetings held by William Branham, Oral Roberts, Loren Fox, and others. In fact, I accepted Christ into my heart as Savior at a young age in a tent revival of Loren Fox in Waukegan, Illinois, in the late forties. I literally walked the "sawdust trail." In many of the meetings we attended, I saw healings that were real. I realize that I was young and impressionable, but in later years, I researched similar physical healings and found them to be truly remarkable and real.

THE TANGENT

As time went by, what had begun as a sovereign move of God went off on a tangent. "Ministries" sprang up with their main focus being physical healing. Healing, healing, healing, and more healing. One very popular "healer" claimed to have the gift of word of knowledge and was supposedly able to tell a person what their infirmity was "supernaturally" and it created quite a stir and following. Later, however, it was discovered to be a sham. Evidently, the evangelist's wife would have people socializing with the audience before the meetings, acting as just another interested attendee, and they would find out personal details as to where they were from, etc., and in the course of the conversation, people from the audience would mention their need for healing in great detail. The interviewers would then report to the evangelist's wife of their findings. During the meeting, she would transmit this information to the evangelist by a wireless microphone to a receiver in the ear of the evangelist describing the appearance of the person, what they were wearing, etc., and the evangelist would then identify them in the audience, call them by name, and share information about them, such as where they were from, and what their need for healing was. He would then lay hands on them, command that sickness to come out of them. They would sometimes be "slain in the Spirit" (fall over backwards to the floor), and after much emotion and rejoicing, testify to be healed, but most of the time it was a temporary emotional high and the illness was still evident. I must admit that, in some cases, a genuine healing was received. Some have suggested that some of the illnesses were psychosomatic, but that is a speculation that I won't go further into at this point.

Other ministries would have "plants" in the audience, who would pretend to be handicapped and would come to the front and be "healed." We could go on and on with examples of quackery that was promoted as Divine healing. Though indeed, sovereign acts of God produced genuine healing, the trickery and excess caused harm to the cause of Christ and many turned away from the Lord as a result of the fakes.

So, does that mean that the gift of healing should not be available to the church today, as some suggest? Does that mean that we cannot believe God for Divine healing in this day and age? If this is true then why is healing listed among the gifts of the Spirit?

There is another concern I have with the promotion of the gift of healing, and it is this: There are many teachings that a Christian is not supposed to be sick. They are supposed to be living in *Divine health* because of Christ's sacrifice on the cross. If sickness comes into the life of a believer, they say it is because of unrepentant sin. It is further promoted that God will *always* heal, He will *never* deny healing if we have the faith to believe. Then that leads to another related problem: Evidently, if a person admits they have pain or suffering after being prayed for, it is said that their healing will be taken away from them due to the lack of faith. Then there is the "*speak the Word*" crowd. This group of people believe that whatever we speak, we get, and that goes hand in hand with the *prosperity-Gospel*. Speak that you can have a new Lexus, and you will have it, etc., etc., etc.

Where is the power of Christ in all of this excess? Where? *It is back in the circle of truth!* God's Holy Word. There *is* provision in that circle for divine physical healing! To deny that is to deny the Word of God. Due to the extreme tangents, what happens? The church is sometimes missing God's blessing for healing because they don't want to be identified with those *fanatics* who are stressing one small part of God's Word to the exclusion of the whole truth given by God. Satan's confusion has robbed the church of God's blessing and he stands by laughing at us!

Most cults have their base in the Word of God, but out of context and away from the whole truth. I have found that you can prove anything you want by quoting the Bible. Did you know that you can prove that there is no God using the Bible? The Bible says so! It says in Psalm 14:1, ". . . there is no God." However, as we check the context of that Scripture, it reads, "The fool has said in his heart, 'There is no God.'" What changed? The context. It really makes a difference when you read the whole verse or the verses leading up to, and following, a doctrinal truth. Often, some of the verses in the Bible begin with "therefore." Before reading the next verse, tie it into the text of the previous verse to find out what "therefore" is there for. To get the context, you may even have to read several verses before and after a point you are questioning. Also, in publications when you see ". . ." before or after a verse, get suspicious. Sometimes it is used correctly, but realize something is missing because it is not critical to the essence of the portion being presented, but, as demonstrated above, it can make a *big* difference. When reading Scripture, please be aware that it was not originally written in chapter and verse format. The divisions were added much later to make it easier to locate certain Scripture passages. Frankly, I don't feel that bible editors or translators were very careful as to where they placed the verse and chapter divisions.

Just because someone quotes Scripture to prove that healing is always God's will, does not mean that it is. Find out what the Bible *really* says, not just a part of a verse here or there but what does the Word say *in context*. Does everyone get healed that is prayed for? No. Does that mean that we should not pray for healing? No. This is not a contradiction. When we pray for healing, we need to pray *according to the will of God*. Sometimes, God chooses to withhold physical healing because He has something greater. The Apostle Paul is believed to have had a physical problem; he called it a "thorn in the flesh." We are not sure what it was. Some say it might have been an eye problem. Anyway, he prayed several times to have this problem healed. God finally said to Paul, "My grace is sufficient for you, for power is perfected in weakness" (1 Corinthians 12). Paul later said that, "...I have learned to be content in whatever circumstances I am in. I know how to get along with humble means, and I also know how to live in prosperity: in any and every circumstance I have learned the secret of being filled and going hungry, both of having abundance and suffering need. I can do all things through Him who strengthen me" (Phil. 4:11-1

Oh, how we need the faith of Paul. Too often we want the "quick fix" and don't have patience to wait for a supernatural healing or for whatever it is that God has for us. When we don't receive an answer instantly, we think, *What a testimony of God's healing power that would be*, and we are disappointed with God. However, it seems that God sometimes has a better idea. Maybe he needs to teach us patience before we receive what we pray for, or perhaps

He brings us something else that proves even better than just physical healing.

I mentioned previously that the Apostle Paul found that God had a greater reason for withholding physical healing. Immediately, my mind goes to a great person of faith in our generation—Joni Eareckson Tada. Many of you might know her story. In her late teens, she became a quadriplegic as a result of an injury during a diving accident. Many believed that God would healer her and accused her of having a lack of faith or that there must be sin in her life, causing her not to receive her healing. It was an extremely trying time for Joni, and she even began to doubt God. Like Job, in the old testament, she had the choice to listen to her critics or simply have faith in God *in her circumstance.* She placed her trust in God! Over the decades that she has lived with her injury, she has blessed many, many people with the testimony of her healing.

I spoke to her after one of her meetings, and while she is still needing a wheelchair and special care for her personal needs, she has had another type of healing. You can see it in her smile and hear it in her voice. Her attitude and character have been totally healed, and as a result, she has helped many people over her lifetime to overcome life's difficult situations. Just think! If God had done it man's way by giving her immediate physical healing, many people would have been robbed of the joy of relying on God through and in difficult situations. And the bonus—she will be totally healed physically as she is able, then, to stand before her Lord and Savior and will have a great reward for her ministry to others. God's way is not always easy, but it is always the best. He knows the beginning till the end for He said in Revelation 22:13, "I am the Alpha and the Omega, the first and the last, the beginning and the end".

There are many other similar situations where God has blessed. I think of Fanny Crosby, the writer of many of our beloved songs of praise who, while missing physical sight, had great insight.

How our hearts have been blessed many times by songs such as *To God Be the Glory, Great Things He Hath Done* and *Praise Him, Praise Him! Jesus, Our Blessed Redeemer*, and many more whose words she penned.

So, let's not miss a blessing from God. If God's plan is to heal physically, accept it. Don't deny it because of some excess tangent or error. I believe that I can speak from experience. In 1998, I had ten cardiac arrests in a three-day period, the longest lasting for four minutes. After much confusion about my condition, it was discovered that my heart was not the problem, rather it was the vagus nerve that had been affected by a stomach ulcer having eaten into the nerve, causing the electrical signal from the brain to not reach the heart to allow it to beat. After several blood transfusions due to extreme loss of blood, they found that some of the blood that I had received was contaminated with hepatitis C (at that time there was no name for it and called it non-A, non-B hepatitis). There was no known cure for it. I was told that I would be a prime candidate for cancer of the liver. A few years after this happened, I was attending a revival meeting hosted by a dear friend and evangelist.

To that point, I had never felt I should ask God for healing, but during the service, I sensed that the Lord was prompting me to ask for prayer. As the evangelist placed his hands on me, I sensed a warmth go through my body, and from that day to this, my liver function tests have been normal. Really, I believe that I received my healing, but according to medical science, I was not allowed to donate blood because hepatitis C had been in my system. Though I felt that I had been healed, I still had hepatitis C according to blood tests. In 2019, after a twelve-week treatment, I am now totally free of hepatitis C. It is no longer in my system. God blessed medical science with a cure!

So, fellow Christian, I have said all of this so that you aren't robbed of God's best for you. If you are suffering from physical problems and desire them to go away, believe that God can, and will, heal you if that is His perfect will for your life. If it is not, He will give you the peace to accept it and will use the problem you suffer from to bless you and others by your testimony. I can't neglect what Paul said to the church in Rome: "And we know that God causes all things to work together for good to those who love God, to those who are called according to His purpose." (Romans 8:28) By the way, read what precedes this verse in Romans 8. Remember, when you see "and" or some other conjunction, these are transition words that refer us to the context of what is just being written or what is to follow (as I have previously noted). In Romans 8: 26 & 27,(prior to verse 28, Paul explains that God encourages how to pray, according to His will for us. Considering this, verse 28 means even more than if we read it by itself. Finally, have faith in God, not faith in *faith*. There is a big difference. Trust God and *know* that God has his best in store for you.

3

PROPHECY

Prophecy is a gift given to the church so that the truth of the Word of God is clearly proclaimed with authority. Some have correctly referred to prophecy as "forthtelling." Often, we think of prophecy as "foretelling" rather than forthtelling. In reality, the whole Bible itself is prophecy for it is written by inspired men of God who were prompted by God to proclaim His message to mankind, for we read in 2 Peter 1:20–21, "But know this first of all, that no prophecy of Scripture is a matter of one's own interpretation, for no prophecy was ever made by an act of human will, but men moved by the Holy Spirit spoke from God." While it is true that some of the Bible is foretelling future events, most of the Bible is simply showing how God relates to man and how man should relate to God. Prophecy, therefore, is basically God communicating with man.

Many people claim to be prophets, but what proof does Scripture have to determine that a prophet is truly from God? There are many, but one very important quality of a true prophet of God is found in Jeremiah 28:9, ". . . when the word of the prophet shall come to pass, then that prophet will be known as one whom the Lord has truly sent." Of course, we are referring here to the foretelling aspect of prophecy. The true test of a prophet of God, then, is that he/she is one hundred percent accurate and dependable. What a prophet is not, is a high and lofty personality that draws attention to himself/herself. While the ministry of pastor/teacher is to equip the church for works of service (Eph. 4:12), in proclaiming the Word of God, they are often functioning as God's prophet to the church, giving the message of God (forthtelling). Some might dispute this, but I am certainly open to discussion on this point.

The ultimate mode of prophecy, as I have already noted, is the written Word of God. One advantage we have today over the old testament and early church believers is that we have the complete cannon of Scripture to guide us, to speak to us, and to help us. The problem facing the church today is that the Bible can't speak to us when it is collecting dust on a shelf at home. The Apostle Paul writing to Timothy, the young pastor and student of Paul, said that he should study the Word (2 Tim. 2:15).

THE TANGENT

In our culture, the word prophet is often used for people who claim to have insight into the future. I am referring now to the individuals outside of the church. Several years ago, a lady by the name of Jean Dixon was often quoted as telling future events. In fact, she used to have a series of predictions at the end of each year for the coming year. Some were extreme and crazy, but some were reasonable. However, most were wrong. She claimed to be a Christian and was very much involved with the Roman Catholic Church, so she was revered by many people. I and most other Christians never considered her a true prophet of God. There have been others of note such as Nostradamus, Edgar Cayce, Ed Dames, Sir Arthur Conan Doyle, and many others that claimed to have the ability to see into the future. Many of those fell into trances, some relied on "spirit guides" (demons), but very few of their prophecies had been fulfilled. Nostradamus wrote verse prophecies called quatrains that are open to many different interpretations. They are like riddles, and can be interpreted many ways. These and such other things as Ouija boards, horoscopes, palm reading, tea leaf reading, etc. are to be avoided by true Christians. They are not only unreliable, but I believe that they are deceptive and demonic, and *none of them* are parts of God's circle of truth.

Since prophecy is listed as a gift of the Spirit in the Bible, and a tangent to the Word of God, it is real and accurate. However, the people that I have given as examples are so off on a tangent that they are not even remotely reliable and must be avoided.

Getting back to the gift of prophecy in the church, it can also get off on a tangent. There are false prophets operating in the church that have a powerful influence in the life of many Christians. Jim Jones was a minister who had a large following. He eventually became extremely authoritarian as a leader and dictated what his members could do or could not do. He claimed he spoke "for God" and that he was God's voice to the congregation, they could not marry without his permission, etc. Of course, we know the end story of him and his followers. They all followed his "godly" advice and moved to South America, and they eventually died, as he instructed them to drink poisoned Kool-Aid. How dreadful and foolish!

The same type of thing, perhaps less extreme, is going on in some churches. People's lives are being controlled by power-hungry, strong personality leaders that claim to be prophets of God. Many cults have developed in this way: starting with the whole counsel of God's Word, then going "off on a tangent," and glorifying themselves rather than God. It is extremely important to make sure that you are in a fellowship of believers that teach and preach the whole counsel of God's Holy Word.

When someone says that they have a word from the Lord for you, gauge what they say by the written Word of God. *God will never disagree with His written Word!* Let me say something else about the *"God told me"* crowd. I was in a pastoral theology class in college, and the professor was talking about this very thing. He cautioned that well-meaning people can often cause confusion when they say that *"God told me . . ."* and then try to guide you in this way. The professor went on to relate a rather humorous incident in his life. It seems that a young lady was attracted to him in his early years as a pastor, and she was somewhat annoying in her pursuit of him. One day, she came up to him and said, very seriously, "God told me that it is His plan that you and I should marry." He was caught off guard and was somewhat surprised. Pausing to think for a moment, he then gently said to the young lady, "Well, this is very interesting. I guess when God tells me the same thing, we will both know what God wants." Needless to say, he wasn't further pursued by this young lady.

Though this has humor in it, it presents a real lesson for us. There may be a situation when God is impressing you regarding His will for your life. It is at these times that a prophetic word might be given to *confirm* what God has revealed to you. Perhaps this could involve vocation or education choices. Perhaps God is calling you into full-time Christian service, and God might use a brother or sister in Christ to confirm what He has tried to reveal to you. Don't, however, be confused by following a direction in your life *just because someone said God told them that you should*. Remember, Jesus is quoted in John 10:27, "My sheep hear My voice, and I know them, and they follow Me." Often, people believe that the only ones that can hear from God are the *super spiritual* Christians. Hear me, please! Let me quickly correct that error. Before you and I became Christians, we *heard from God*. We recognized that the Holy Spirit of God was calling us to Him. John 6:44 says, "No one can come to Me unless the Father who sent Me draws him; and I will raise him up on the last day" To come to Jesus for salvation, you heard the voice of God drawing you to Him. Why can you not also listen to His voice for guidance? I'm not talking about an audible voice, but rather, that still small voice of God.

In closing this topic, I want to offer a further word of caution. As we have the written Word of God to guide us, we need *to heavily* rely on His Word, the Bible, for confirmation. The gift of prophecy and the other gifts are there to encourage the church, but they should *never* supersede the authority of the Scriptures. When they do, we will find ourselves hopelessly "off on a tangent."

4

HOLINESS

It is difficult to place priorities on extreme tangents, but, in my opinion, the theme of holiness should rank near the top. It seems to be extremely misunderstood and has caused many to become discouraged because they feel that they can't be "holy enough" to please God.

In the mid-nineteenth and early twentieth centuries, there was an awakening in the North American Church to the need for greater emphasis on holiness. Great men of God such as D.L. Moody, Billy Sunday, and others were instrumental in a great move of God. Many felt that the so-called "mainline denominations" had lost their vision for holiness and were drifting further and further away from encouraging holiness. There seemed to be a form of godliness, but no evidence of God's power.

This gave rise to what became known as the "Holiness movement." At first, Christians from various denominations began gathering together for fellowship and worship and eventually organized what we refer to as the holiness churches. One of the first was the Pentecostal Church of the Nazarene (which later dropped "Pentecostal" from their name). The Wesleyan Methodist Church, Pilgrim Holiness Church, The Assemblies of God, and many others were formed. Many of these were "Pentecostal" in doctrine, believing in the ability to pray in unknown languages. Some were not, but all were committed to the theme of holiness. I was raised in the holiness environment of that time.

The main emphasis was to live a life pleasing to God. A great missionary movement was begun and still exists today as a result of the dedication of those early years of God's sovereign move and anointing. Much emphasis was placed on living pure and holy lives. Some even went to the extreme, saying that after receiving Christ as Savior, you must seek the infilling of the Holy Spirit. Of course, it is hard to prove the need for a second work of grace (infilling of the Holy Spirit), but many embraced that doctrine, and still do today. In Ephesians 5:18, Paul instructs the church to "be filled with the Spirit." Now, where does he mention the second work of grace? He is telling us to be filled with the Spirit. It is not a one-time experience subsequent to salvation but should be an ongoing conscious recognition to seek a daily, moment by moment infilling of the precious Holy Spirit. Paul further states in Galatians 5:24–26, "Now those who belong to Christ Jesus have crucified the flesh with its passions and desires. If we live by the Spirit, let us also walk by the Spirit. Let us not become boastful, challenging one another, envying one another." It was taught that if you are God's servant then let Him live through you to produce holiness in your life. It was preached that when you became a born again Christian, your spirit became the dwelling place of Christ, and was holy and separated to God.

Allow me to digress for a moment and further explain this. The soul and body, should ultimately display that same purity as the inner man, namely spirit, where God's Holy Spirit dwells, allowing the Christian to overcome the "desires of the flesh." I am convinced that the spirit of man is dead because of sin, but has been made perfect in the believer, because it is the dwelling place of God, as if it were His new Holy of Holies. The spirit of the Christian is as holy as it will ever be because it is the habitation of God, and "what fellowship has light with darkness?" (2 Corinthians 6:14) Some would argue that the carnal nature and the spiritual nature of the Christian are both residents in the spirit of man. Based on what I have just stated, I am convinced that the old nature was always part of the soul (emotion, intellect) of man because the spirit of man died with the sin of Adam and Eve. That is why we needed to be born again as Jesus explains to Nicodemus in John, Chapter 3. That could also explain why, in the old testament, the Spirit of God was *with* man but was never mentioned as indwelling man because the spirit of man was dead because of sin. Therefore, unless we are allowing the infilling of the Holy Spirit, our carnal nature can starve the vibrancy and the joy in our Christian walk. Our whole Christian life can be a life of defeat and misery. I tend to be convinced that we will not lose our salvation, but we will certainly not have an overcoming, victorious Christian life because we do not allow God's Spirit to control our old nature. Admittedly, many are not in agreement with this; be that as it may, there have been many spirited discussions as to whether or not a person can lose his/her salvation, but many Christians are in agreement with the doctrine of eternal security, and we can agree to disagree.

I recently heard a well-known minister say that he believes in eternal security, but not *unconditional* eternal security. I think I know where he is coming from with this, and I tend to agree.

Getting back to our previous topic, over time, in the Holiness movement, the emphasis seemed to become more and more on externals. There were lists of sins that one should not commit, and if you did, you weren't holy, or worse yet, not even a Christian.

Please note: Legalism is not Godliness! Jesus spoke against the lifestyle of the Pharisees. He said in Matthew 23:27–28, "Woe to you, scribes and Pharisees, hypocrites, For you are like whitewashed tombs which on the outside appear beautiful, but inside they are full of dead men's bones and all uncleanness. Even so you too outwardly appear righteous to men, but inside, they are full of hypocrisy and lawlessness." This was true and is still sound doctrine, touching the circle of truth. We need to be holy.

Over time, however, the emphasis became more and more on externals. There were lists of sins that one could not commit, and if you did, you weren't holy. What had begun as a genuine move of God's holiness, by some, became a legalistic system of "do this and don't do that."

Obviously, legalism is *not* holiness!

As I previously mentioned, I was raised in a holiness church, and God instilled in me a lifelong appreciation for true holiness. I considered what I was being taught as normal and correct, but I began to see problems. One time, we had a combined church service with a neighboring church of a different denomination, but still considered a holiness church. Following the service, on the way home, the conversation in the car drifted to the preacher's wife and the fact that she had lipstick on and was wearing flashy jewelry. You see, our "list" on holiness was that our ladies did not wear makeup or flashy jewelry. Holy people just did not do that!

I was also raised to believe that owning a TV was sinful, and it was a tool of the devil, so we did not have a TV. As you read on, you will see that TV was eventually accepted. I used to come home from school and lie on the floor in front of the radio and listen to my favorite radio shows such as *The Adventures of Sky King*, *Sergeant Preston and the Royal Mounted Police*, *Bobbie Benson and the B Bar B Ranch*, and many, many others. During the day, Mom used to do her housework while listening to soap operas like *Backstage Wife*, *Stella Dallas*, *Pepper Young's Family*, and others. The reason I am mentioning these is that in the 1940s, in radio's infancy, radio was also considered "worldly" and "sinful" and should not be allowed in a life of holiness.

Getting back to "sinful TV," In the 50s I used to go to the neighbor's each Saturday morning to watch cartoons and other kids programs. This bothered my dad, even though the preacher said TV was wrong, to avoid confusing our neighbors as to our "religion," he eventually bought a 17" Motorola TV, radio, phonograph console and had them installed in our house. This replaced the old radio console. He made sure that the TV had doors on it to cover it in case the preacher ever came to visit. The preacher would just think it was a radio/phonograph console (which was common in the 1950s). Looking back, it seems comical. Let me add another wrinkle, even stranger: The neighboring town of Racine, Wisconsin, had a church of our denomination, and the pastor was facing the same problem with the needs of his teenage son going to the neighbor's to watch TV, so the pastor also purchased a TV. Now, back in those days, you needed to have a huge antenna on the roof to get TV reception. The parsonage (pastor's house) was located next door to the church, so to avoid a problem with people seeing an antenna on the parsonage, he had it installed inside the church steeple and ran the antenna wire to the parsonage. Problem solved!

Our neighborhood kids used to play together and were very close friends with each other. I liked to play marbles, and so did they, so we were enjoying ourselves when my parents found out that I was playing for "keeps." What do I mean by that? In "keeps," the winner of the round would keep all the marbles played. In "funs," each player would remember which marbles they played and get them back after the round. My parents said that playing for "keeps" was gambling, at least that is what the pastor had said. So, I could only play for "funs." That wasn't too bad. I was bothered by something else, though. Many Saturdays, the neighborhood kids would get together and take the city bus to our local theater. One day, they were planning to go see the movie *Snow White and the Seven Dwarfs*, a popular Disney movie. As usual, I could not go with them because movies were not allowed. They were "sinful." I remember one particular day, sitting on the curb, watching them board the bus and excited to see this Disney movie. One of the mothers was seeing everyone off when she noticed me sitting there. "Bobby," she asked, "aren't you going to see the movie with other kids?" When I replied "no," she wanted to know why. I simply said, "It's against my religion to go to shows." I vividly remember her rolling her eyes and walking back to her house without saying another word.

There were many other things in my childhood that confused me. I remember when my uncle, John, was visiting from Indianapolis, Indiana. We were seated at the supper table, and I noticed in the newspaper lying there that there was a circus coming to town, and I got excited and asked Mom if we could go. Well, Uncle John, being a staunch Nazarene, simply looked at me and said, "Son, a carnival is a little devil, but a circus is a big devil." That seemed odd to me. I could mention several other incidents in my early childhood and teen years that confused me, but I think I have offered enough to show the ignorance that changed "holiness" into "legalism." I don't want to paint with too broad of a brush, however. True holiness was still practiced, but to a larger extent, holiness was becoming legalism.

The reason I have spent time on this is to illustrate that this was all many people thought that holiness was . . . Simply a list of what we can and cannot do and if we live by our list we are living a holy life. What does the Bible say about holiness? Let's look at Hebrews 12:14 (NEV) which reads, *"Work at living in peace with everyone and work at living a holy life for those who are not holy will not see the Lord."* If holiness is not just a list of what we can and cannot do, then *what is holiness?* Simply put, holiness is separation. Separation from sin and all that is ungodly. Really? It sounds impossible and unrealistic to live that way! If you are inclined to feel this way then you are absolutely correct! It is impossible for anyone who has not been born again, or for a "born again" believer living by the dictates of the old sinful nature, to live a life of holiness. The world and the flesh cannot understand the things of God for they are *spiritually discerned.* (see 1 Cor. 2:14)

The nature of a human being is to live a life for self. Man has a very selfish nature and cannot understand the things of God. The new nature of the believer is to please God in all things. When we accept Jesus as Savior, His Holy Spirit takes residence in our spirit. Our goal is then to allow Christ to conform our nature to His nature. Paul says in 2 Cor. 3:18, "But we all, with unveiled faces, looking as in a mirror at the glory of the Lord, are being transformed into the same image from glory to glory, just as from the Lord, the Spirit." 1 Peter 1:16 also says, "because it is written, YOU SHALL BE HOLY, FOR I AM HOLY" (Paul is quoting here from Lev. 11:44).

It seems, then, that we as Christians cannot please God without holiness. Holiness is not a list of rules we try to live by, but holiness is allowing God's Spirit, dwelling in our spirit, to transform us from *within*. We are told in the Word that man looks on and considers the outward things but God looks inside at the heart. Apart from the leading of the Spirit of God, then, man tries to form a religious system with externals . . . do this . . . don't do that, etc. Christ, however, living in the believer, desires to have the outward man conform to what He has already done to the spirit of man. God wants to make us holy and live holy lives because of His Holy presence within us! For further study, I suggest that you read Roman 7 and 8. Paul makes it very clear in these passages of Scripture regarding the battle between the old and the new nature, and the victory we have to live overcoming lives for Him.

THE TANGENT

As long as we are in God's Circle of Ttruth, holiness is scriptural, and necessary, if we are to live a life pleasing to the Lord. As long as we are in God's Circle of Truth, we are OK. It is when we get "off on a tangent" with holiness that it simply becomes legalism. Legalism is pride personified that causes us to become judgmental and critical of someone not living up to our standards. Legalism is simply the old sinful nature trying to control our lives. Legalism is the cause of so many church splits. Legalism has contributed to the world getting a totally wrong picture of what the church is and what it represents. The world looks at the legalistic Christian with all of the fault finding and arguing and says, "I don't need that. I have enough problems without adding religion to my life. It's not for me!"

We can say it another way: Legalism is religion or man trying to be good enough to reach God. Holiness is Christ reaching to man to bring him into fellowship with God. Let's seek after holiness as we enjoy living victorious Christian lives in God's circle of truth.

5

PRAISE AND WORSHIP

This may seem like a strange topic when it comes to tangent teachings, but I am convinced that it is a very important theme for the church today. Praise is one of the most important ministries of the Christian Church, for it is our acknowledgment of all that Christianity is. It is the expression of our love and devotion to God. Offering praise and worship is vital to our relationship with God. This theme is so vast that I really can't do it justice with just a brief chapter in this book, but hopefully, with God's help, I can spark something in the life of the believer that will prompt further study in this very important topic.

Some suggest that Lucifer was originally created to be the praise and music leader in heaven, based on Ezekiel 28:13. This has been debated and will continue to be a topic of debate until the end of the age when the church will finally be with Jesus. Whether or not this was the original purpose for Lucifer's existence, we know that he rebelled against God and led a third of the angels in heaven to rebel with him, causing Lucifer and his followers to be expelled from heaven. Since this book is dealing with tangents and not a detailed Bible history, I suggest that you "Google" this theme if you want more details. Suffice it to say, Lucifer was, and is, against God and God's people, and it is his desire to destroy the church through confusion and any other means that he can use to do so. I will attempt to show you how he is using the theme of praise and worship to attempt to accomplish his goal.

Before we get into that, let us consider what the Bible says about praise and worship. BibleGateway.com, a web-based Scripture search program, recognizes 254 Bible verses that deal with worship and 263 verses that deal with praise, making a total of 517 in which praise and/or worship are mentioned. While some are probably dealing with both praise and worship that could make the total number of verses less, it is still a lot that the bible says about the topic, so it must be important.

Let's look into it a little deeper. Here are just a sampling of Scripture verses dealing with praise and worship: "My lips will shout for joy when I sing praises to You; And my soul which You have redeemed." (Psalm 71:23) "Enter His gates with thanksgiving And His courts with praise. Give thanks to Him, bless His name." (Psalm 100:4) "Sing to the Lord a new song, sing His praise from the end of the earth." (Isaiah 42:10) "Through Him then, let us continually offer up a sacrifice of praise to God, that is, the fruit of the lips that give thanks to His name." (Hebrews 13:15) "Ascribe to the Lord the glory due His name; Worship the Lord in holy array." (Psalm 29:2) "And all the angels were standing around the throne and *around* the elders and around the four living creatures; and they fell on their faces before the throne and worshiped God." (Revelation 7:11)

God inhabits the praises of His people (Ps. 22:3). He made man to fellowship with Him, and we see in Genesis that He daily visited man in the Garden of Eden, and God still desires fellowship with His children, and He wants to bless us. What we call the book of Psalms, really, was originally mostly hymns of praise and thanksgiving. It was evidently common for people under the old covenant to praise the Lord through music, and even to do so using musical instruments such as the harp and lyre, among others. In the new testament, the Apostle Paul reminds us to praise the Lord with hymns and spiritual songs (Col. 3:16). In modern times, hymns and spiritual choruses have been a regular part of a worship service as the congregation blends their voices in vocal corporate worship.

In our modern era, the secular entertainment industry has taken giant steps to provide recorded music and videos so that we are never in a situation, it seems, where we cannot be entertained. Many recorded albums are available through stores or downloads as recorded by popular bands and vocal groups, etc. Radio and television came on the scene in the twentieth century, changing forever our way of life. Worldwide "live" programs are streamed into our homes by satellite on a regular basis. What the industry has discovered (or possibly created) is that modern mankind "needs" to be entertained. We see it in all areas of life. Even our cell phones entertain us with video and audio.

The church and parachurch have not been without involvement in this modern entertainment process. We have been blessed with Christian radio twenty-four-hour programing in most markets. It is a blessing to be able to have uplifting Christian music almost anywhere we go. There are many committed Christian artists blessing the church through this venue, and I pray that they will continue to minister with their anointed music. But we have noticed a downside to what is happening, too. I also see a disturbing trend of secular artists, seeing an opportunity to capitalize on this, becoming involved in the Christian entertainment business, making a name for themselves, and in many cases turning what has been praise gatherings into purely entertainment venues, with much of the same sounds and sights that the secular concerts have. I then see the Christian artists trying to compete with this, and, as a result, their ministry has suffered. Oh, don't get me wrong. They are being successful and drawing great crowds to their concerts, but what has happened to "praise and worship?" In many cases, these concerts are simply entertainment just like the secular rock concerts. It seems that we have allowed the enemy, Satan, to invade what was once a sacred and special time of honoring Jesus through praise and worship and turn it into something of the world, not of Christ. I'm not just talking about the beat of the music, or the lighting, or anything like that. I'm talking about the anointing of the Holy Spirit that seems to be missing, about the heart honoring the Lord and allowing control His life-changing Spirit. As we worship around the throne in heaven, can we expect it to be like a rock concert or will it be a solemn time when millions of us fall on our faces before the King of Kings and honor Him with our honest worship and praise?

What is the response of the church to the modern secular music marvel? Some churches feel that they have to compete. Many secular ideas and themes are being incorporated into the worship services to grab the attention of the youth. To be fair, some churches are using these techniques, but not to the exclusion of allowing the Holy Spirit to minister to the needs of the people. There are some churches, however, who seem to have abandoned the ministry and have just become places of entertainment. They turn the auditorium lights down or off, and spotlight and highlight the performers. The audience seems to be there to view and not to be a part of the worship.

We must realize that God is changeless. What appeals to our flesh is not necessarily what pleases God. In 2 Samuel 6, we have an incident when it was decided to move the ark of the covenant back to Israel after many years. God had very plain instructions as to how the ark was to be traveled. If His instruction were not followed, it would result in tragedy and death.

It seems that someone thought of a better, more modern way, to move the ark. The instructions had been to have priests bear the ark on poles placed through brackets on each side of the ark. Evidently, this was too old fashioned for this move. They built a cart and placed the ark on the cart. It seemed more efficient to do it that way. Well, on the way back to Jerusalem, the ark seemed unstable and it looked like it might fall off of the cart, so a man named Uzzah saw what was happening and simply reached up and touched the ark to stabilize it. He was instantly killed, for no one but God's appointed servants could deal with the ark. God's way is always God's way. We may think that we have a better idea, but if we are not careful, we can grieve God and suffer the consequences. God's way to move the ark was the only safe way to do so.

What does this have to do with praise and worship? There is no record in the Bible that tells us that praise and worship were intended to be entertainment for the people. It was strictly to be for God, and since God inhabits the praises of His people, as previously noted, God is pleased to bless the people as they worship Him in spirit and in truth. It seems that in our quest to become modern and "hip," we have sometimes created a *new cart*. We seem to be using Hollywood and Nashville techniques to enhance the experience for the worshipers. It is thought that this is the only way we can increase or even maintain our numbers at worship services. John 12:32 says, "And I, if I am lifted up from the earth, will draw all men to Myself." Matt. 6:33 further states "But Seek first His kingdom and His righteousness, and all these things shall be provided to you."

THE TANGENT

As we exalt Jesus Christ, we will see God's Spirit move in our midst. Scripture says that we are to praise God with hymns and spiritual songs that exalt the name and character of the

Lord. When we drift from that, we can easily get "off on a tangent" and not be in the center of God's will and purpose. We must always remember to stay with the basics, the circle of truth, and not go "off on a tangent."

CONCLUSION

While I have only begun to talk about the many areas that we can be "off on a tangent," I hope that this has whetted your appetite in this area of tangents, and that you will see if there are other tangents in your life that need to touch God's Circle of Truth.

We cannot be truly successful in our Christian walk if we are not living in God's Circle of Truth. As we find ourselves going off on various tangents, not supported by the "whole counsel" of God's Word, we will not experience the joy of the Lord that God has for us. Would you rather sit at a table and enjoy the full meal or just be satisfied with what falls to the floor as part of the meal? Wouldn't you rather have your plate full with the whole meal and a good beverage along with a satisfying dessert? Perhaps that is oversimplifying the point; however, to be fully nourished, we need the whole counsel of God's Word, not bits and pieces.

Let's pull up to God's table and enjoy all of what He has for us.

CPSIA information can be obtained
at www.ICGtesting.com
Printed in the USA
BVHW041928020322
630506BV00019B/510

9 781649 907745